Guess What!

Student's Book 3

American English

Susannah Reed with Kay Bentley

Series Editor: Lesley Koustaff

CAMBRIDGE
UNIVERSITY PRESS

Contents

Welcome

Guess What!

1 (CD1 02) **Listen and point.**

2 (CD1 03) **Listen, point, and repeat.**

3 (CD1 04) **Listen and say the names.**

4 (Think) **Describe and guess who.**

She's four years old.   Anna!

1 Lucas
2 Max
3 Lily
4 Tom
5 Anna

5 (CD1 05) **Sing the song.**

Questions,
questions ...

Questions, questions,
I like asking questions.
What's your name?
How old are you?
What's your favorite color?

Questions, questions,
I like asking questions.
Do you like sports?
Do you have a pet?
Can you draw a picture of me?

Questions, questions,
I like asking questions.

6 **Match the questions to the answers.**

1 What's your name?

2 How old are you?

3 What's your favorite color?

4 Do you like sports?

5 Do you have a pet?

6 Can you draw a picture of me?

a Yes, I do. I have a dog.

b I'm ten years old.

c Yes, I do. My favorite sports are swimming and tennis.

d Yes, I can. I like art.

e My name's Lily.

f My favorite color is yellow.

7 (About Me) **Ask and answer with a friend.**

What's your favorite color?   My favorite color is blue.

8 (CD1 06) **Listen and repeat.**

January

February

March

April

May

June

July

August

September

October

November

December

9 (CD1 07) **Listen and say the next month.**

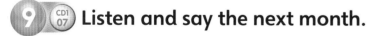

January, February, March ...   April!

10 (About Me) **Ask and answer with a friend.**

When's your birthday?   It's in June.

Remember!

When's your birthday?
It's in December.

11 (CD1 08) **Go to page 102. Listen and repeat the chant.**

Skills: *Reading and speaking*

 Let's start! **Do you have an email pen pal?**

12 CD1 09 **Read and listen.**

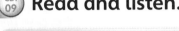

> Hi. My name's Juan. I'm ten years old.
> My birthday is in March.
>
> I live in a small house with my family.
> I have two sisters and a brother. I don't
> have any pets, but I like animals.
>
> I like basketball and field hockey, but
> my favorite sport is baseball. I like
> fishing, too.
>
> What about you?
>
> Email me back.
>
> Juan

13 Read again and answer the questions.

1 How old is Juan?
2 When's his birthday?
3 How many brothers does he have?
4 Does he like animals?
5 Does he like sports?

14 About Me **Ask and answer with a friend.**

How old are you?
Do you have any brothers or sisters?
Do you have a pet?
What's your favorite sport?

Writing

→ Workbook page 7: Write an email to a pen pal.

Listen and repeat. Then act.

fly this kite   do this treasure hunt   go to the movie theater
play outside   go to the sports center

1

Can I play outside, please?

Yes, of course.

2

Can we go to the sports center, please?

No, I'm sorry, you can't.

Say it!

17 Listen and repeat.

Snakes make trails with their tails.

snake

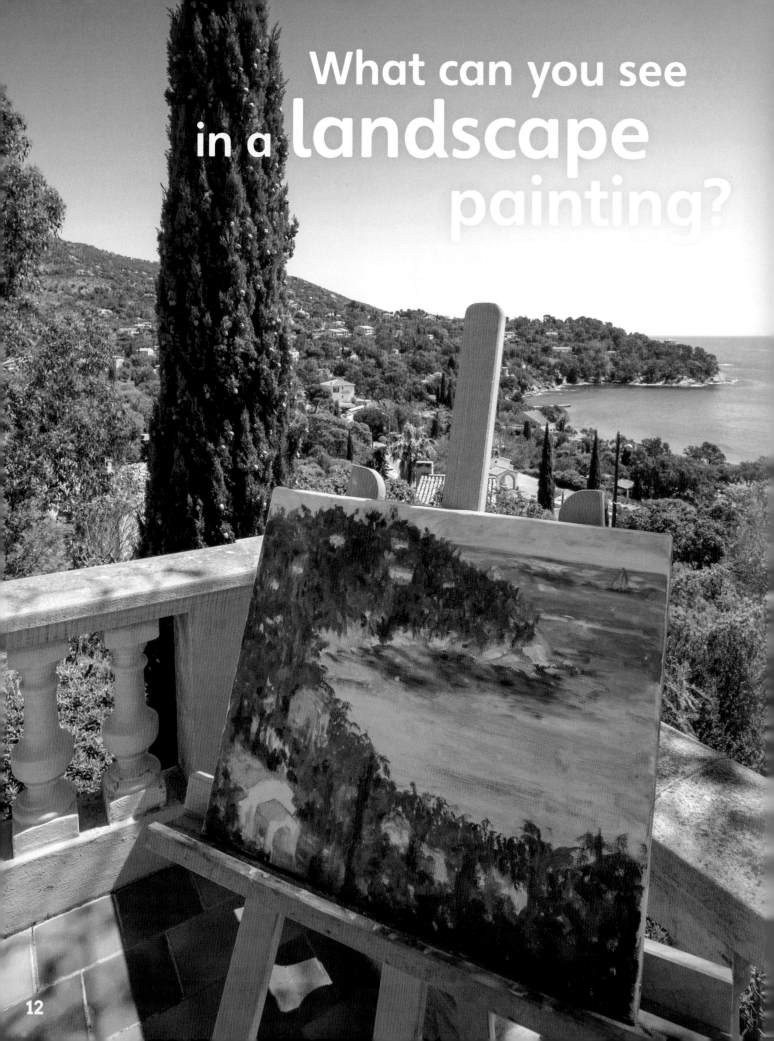

What can you see in a landscape painting?

1 CD1 13 **Listen and repeat.**

① river ② ocean ③ waterfall ④ forest ⑤ mountain

2 **Watch the video.**

3 **What can you see in the landscape paintings?**

 ①

 ②

 ③

 ④

Guess What!

Chinese artists paint landscapes on rice paper and silk.

Project

5 **Make a fact file about a famous landscape artist.**

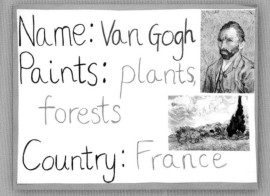

Name: Van Gogh
Paints: plants, forests
Country: France

4 **What would you like to paint in a landscape painting?**

1 In the yard

Guess What!

1 (CD1 14) **Listen and point.**

2 (CD1 15) **Listen, point, and repeat.**

3 (CD1 16) **Listen and say the words.**

4 (Think) **Describe and guess what.**

It's a plant. It's green.   Grass!

1. tree
2. leaf
3. caterpillar
4. rabbit
5. butterfly
6. flower
7. grass
8. turtle
9. guinea pig
10. snail

5 (CD1 17) Sing the song.

My pet is white.
Your pet is gray.
Our pets aren't big,
They're small.
Where are our pets?
Can you see our pets?

Her pet is white.
His pet is gray.
Their pets aren't big,
They're small.
Where are their pets?
Can you see their pets?

Where are our pets?

Can you see their pets?

6 Read and match. Then say the animal.

1

My pet is big and black.

2

Her pet is small and orange.

3

Our pet is small and yellow.

4

Their pet is gray and beautiful.

a

b

c

d

7 Look at the photographs. Ask and answer with a friend.

Number 3. Is their pet a bird?   Yes, it is.

Remember!

His pet is big.
Our pet is orange.

8 (CD1 18) **Listen and repeat.**

1

What's that?

It's a snail.

2

What are those?

They're butterflies.

9 (CD1 19) **Listen and say the numbers.**

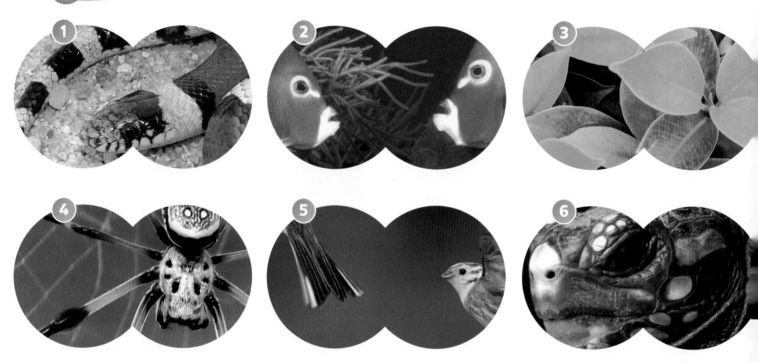

10 **Look at the photographs.**
Ask and answer with a friend.

11 (CD1 20) **Go to page 102. Listen and repeat**
the chant.

Remember!

What's that?
It's a snake.
What are those?
They're leaves.

→ Workbook page 14

Skills: *Listening and speaking*

Let's start! What can you see at the zoo?

12 (CD1 21) **Listen and match.**

House of bugs

a

b

c

d

1 Lucy

2 Ryan

3 Sara

4 Jake

13 (CD1 21) **Listen again and say *true* or *false*.**

1 Lucy likes snails.
2 Ryan likes ants.
3 Sara doesn't like the butterfly.
4 Jake doesn't like caterpillars.

14 (About Me) **Ask and answer with a friend.**

What is your favorite bug?
What color is it?
What bugs can you see outside?

Writing

➡ **Workbook page 15: Write about your favorite bug.**

15 CD1 22 **Read and listen.**

1
What's that?

Max loves soccer.

It's a message!

2
Find a toy tiger.

3
A toy tiger? Where?

Can I help?

Not now, Anna.

4
Look! Behind that tree! What's that?

Are those ears and a tail?

Yes! Come on!

5
Oh! It's a cat!

I can help …

Not now, Anna.

6
Wait! Is this your tiger, Anna?

Yes, it is.

Can we borrow it, please?

7
Yes, you can! Here you are.

Thank you, Anna.

Sorry, Anna. Thank you.

Value: Respect and listen to others

→ Workbook page 16

16 CD1 23 Talk Time Listen and repeat. Then act.

computer game   toy car   eraser   camera   book

1

Can I borrow your camera, please?

Yes, you can.

2

Can I borrow your book, please?

No, I'm sorry, you can't.

Say it!

17 CD1 24 Listen and repeat.

Chimpanzees eat and sleep in trees.

chimpanzee

What types of **habitats** are there?

1 CD1 25 **Listen and repeat.**

desert   rain forest   grassland   tundra

2 **Watch the video.**

3 **Match the habitats with the groups of animals.**

1
monkey
crocodile
snake

2
lion
giraffe
snake

Guess What!

Deserts can be hot and cold. Antarctica is a desert.

desert
grassland
rain forest
tundra

3
spider
snake
camel

4
goat
sheep
bear

Project

5 **Make a mind map for a habitat in your country.**

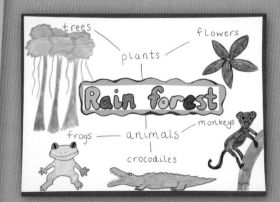

4 **What type of habitat would you like to visit?**

2 At school

Guess What!

1  **Listen and point.**

2 **Listen, point, and repeat.**

Welcome to Forest School

1 reception
2 cafeteria
3 library
4 classroom
5 science lab
6 gym
7 art room
8 music room
9 playground
10 sports field

3 **Listen and say the places.**

4 Think **Describe and guess where.**

This is Lily's favorite room.

Music room!

5 CD1 29 Sing the song.

Dave and Daisy, where are you?
We're in the cafeteria.
Where are Dave and Daisy?
They're in the cafeteria.

Max and Mary, where are you?
We're in the music room.
Where are Max and Mary?
They're in the music room.

Sam and Susie, where are you?
We're on the sports field.
Where are Sam and Susie?
They're on the sports field.

6 Read and match.

 **1**

 **2**

 **3**

a We're in the art room. **b** We're on the playground. **c** We're in the library.

7 Look at the pictures in activities 5 and 6. Ask and answer with a friend.

Where are they?

They're on the playground.

Remember!

Where **are** they?
They're **on the sports field.**

8 CD1 30 **Listen and repeat.**

1

What are you doing?

We're playing tennis.

2

What are they doing?

They're playing tennis.

9 CD1 31 **Look and find. Then listen and say the numbers.**

1 **2** **3** **4** **5**

10 **Look at the picture. Ask and answer with a friend.**

What are they doing?

They're playing baseball.

Remember!

What **are** you do**ing**?
We're play**ing** baseball.

11 CD1 32 **Go to page 102. Listen and repeat the chant.**

Skills: *Reading and speaking*

Let's start! **What places can you find in your school?**

12 CD1 33 **Read and listen. Then match.**

1 My name's Lisa. Can you find a photograph of me? I'm standing outside my school. My school is big.

2 This is the playground. It's a big playground. Some children are playing a game of basketball. I like basketball, but my favorite sport is tennis.

3 This is a classroom. There's a board and some desks and chairs. These children are doing math. I like math, but my favorite class is art. I like drawing and painting.

4 This is my favorite room. It's our school library. There are lots of books, and I like reading. There are a lot of children in the library today.

a

b

c

d

13 **Read again and answer the questions.**

1 Is Lisa's school big or small?
2 What is Lisa's favorite sport?
3 What are the children in the classroom doing?
4 Does Lisa like reading?

14 About Me **Make sentences about your school. Say *true* or *false*.**

Our school is small.   False. It's big.

Writing

 Workbook page 23: Write a description of your school.

16   **Listen and repeat. Then act.**

pick up this litter   clean the living room   play nicely
put those toys in your room

Can I help you?

Yes. Can you clean the living room, please?

Yes, of course.

Thank you.

Say it!

17 **Listen and repeat.**

Tigers sometimes fight at night.

tigers

What materials can we recycle?

1 **CD1 37** **Listen and repeat.**

recycling bin   paper   can   bottle   cardboard

2 **Watch the video.**

3 **What can you recycle?**

Guess What!

We can make recycled paper into paint.

Project

5 Make a colorful placemat from recycled cardboard.

4 **What materials does your school recycle?**

→ Workbook page 26

CLIL: Science **33**

Review

Units 1 and 2

1 Find the months in the word puzzles.

Oct	ruary
Ju	ober
Feb	ember
Sept	ne

Carnival Day

2 Listen and match the months to the photographs.

Sports Day

3 Look at each photograph. Answer the questions.

1 Where are they?
2 What are they doing?

Children's Day

4 Make your own word puzzles for your friend.

Choose months, nature, or places in school:
butter   rary
lib   fly

Teacher's Day

→ Workbook pages 28–29

5 Play the game.

Start

What's that?   It's a rabbit. Good. I have a rabbit.

What are those?   They're spiders. I don't have spiders.

35

3 School days

Guess
What!

1 [CD1 39] **Listen and point.**

2 [CD1 40] **Listen, point, and repeat.**

My week

❶ Mon	❷ Tues
❸ Wed	❹ Thurs — a- apple, b- banana
❺ Fri	❻ Sat — club
❼ Sun — club	

My week ☺

Mon	Tues
Wed	Thurs
Fri	Sat — club
Sun — club	

3 [CD1 41] **Listen and say the days.**

4 (Think) **Make sentences and guess the days.**

He has math, and she has science.

Monday!

❶ Monday
❷ Tuesday
❸ Wednesday
❹ Thursday
❺ Friday
❻ Saturday
❼ Sunday

5 CD1 42 **Sing the song.**

We have math on Monday.
We don't have math on Tuesday.
Do we have math on Wednesday?
Yes, we do – on Wednesday, too.
We have math on Monday and Wednesday.

We have English on Thursday.
We don't have English on Friday.
Do we have English on Monday?
Yes, we do – on Monday, too.
We have English on Monday and Thursday.

6 **Make a schedule with a friend. Ask and answer.**

Do we have science on Monday?

No, we don't. We have science on Tuesday.

7 (About Me) **Make sentences about your schedule. Say *true* or *false*.**

We have music on Monday and Friday.

False!

We don't have music on Wednesday.

True!

Remember!
Do we have science on Tuesday?
Yes, we do.   No, we don't.

8 (CD1 43) **Listen and look. Then listen and repeat.**

Amy

in the morning

lunchtime

in the afternoon

dinnertime

after school

9 **Now read and answer the questions.**

Amy has math and English in the morning.

1 What classes does Amy have in the morning?
2 What classes does Amy have in the afternoon?
3 What club does Amy have after school?
4 What class does Amy have before lunch?
5 What class does Amy have after lunch?

10 **Choose a day from your schedule. Play a guessing game.**

What do you have in the morning?

I have math and science.

Is it Wednesday?

Yes, it is.

11 (CD1 44) **Go to page 102. Listen and repeat the chant.**

Remember!
What club **does she have** after school?
She has swimming club after school.

Skills: *Listening and speaking*

Let's start! **Do you have a favorite day of the week?**

12 (CD1 45) **Listen and choose.**

Caleb

Favorite day
Sunday

Morning
Swimming competition

Afternoon
Art club

Evening
Movie theater trip

Favorite day
Saturday

Morning
Art competition

Afternoon
Movie theater trip

Evening
Dance club

Salima

Favorite day
Friday

Morning
Math test

Afternoon
Field trip to a farm

Evening
Field hockey club

Maddie

13 (CD1 45) **Listen again and say *true* or *false*.**

1 Caleb's favorite class is math.
2 Salima's favorite class is music.
3 Maddie likes playing field hockey.
4 Salima likes dancing.

14 (About Me) **Ask and answer with a friend.**

What's your favorite class?
What clubs do you have after school?
Do you like competitions?
Do you like school tests?

Writing

➜ Workbook page 33: Write about your favorite day.

15 (CD1 46) **Read and listen.**

1 Find this painting.

2 What day is today?

It's Saturday.

Great! I like art. Let's go to the art gallery.

3 Is the art gallery open on Saturdays?

Yes, it is.

Come on. Let's go!

4 OK. Here we are.

Now where's the painting?

Over there!

5 What can we do now?

We can't take a photograph of the painting.

I have an idea!

6 Be careful!

Are you OK, Tom?

Yes, I'm fine. Don't worry.

7 It's very good, Tom.

What do you think, Max?

Listen and repeat. Then act.

art gallery   hospital   sports center   movie theater   library

1 Is the movie theater open on Sundays?

Yes, it is.

2 Is the library open on Mondays in the afternoon?

No, it isn't. It's closed.

Say it!

17 Listen and repeat.

Goats need warm coats in the snow.

goat

Which **animals** are **nocturnal?**

1 CD1 49 **Listen and repeat.**

| koala | fox | bat | scorpion | owl |

2 **Watch the video.**

3 **Which animals are nocturnal?**

Guess What!

At night, owls can see mice 18 m in front of them.

Project

5 Make a fact file about a nocturnal animal.

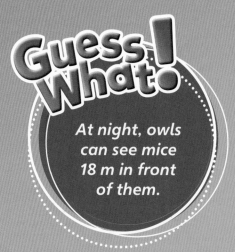

Animal: Koala
Country: Australia
Color: brown
Size: 70–90 cm
At night it eats food.
It can climb trees.

4 **Which animals in your country are nocturnal?**

→ Workbook page 36

4 My day

5 (CD1 53) **Sing the song.**

I get up at 🕗 eight o'clock.
I have breakfast at 🕣 eight thirty.
I go to school at 🕘 nine o'clock,
And I have lunch at 🕧 twelve thirty.
Hey, hey, every day.

I go home at 🕞 three thirty,
And I play with my friends.
I have dinner at 🕢 seven thirty.
I go to bed at 🕘 nine o'clock at night.
Hey, hey, every day.

6 (CD1 54) **Listen and say the names.**

Emily

Sophie

Josh

Jacob

7 (About Me) **Make sentences about your day. Say _true_ or _false_.**

I have breakfast at twelve thirty.

False!

Remember!
I have dinner at seven thirty.
I go to bed at nine o'clock.

8 (CD1 55) **Listen and repeat.**

What time do you have breakfast?

I have breakfast at eight o'clock.

So do I.

I don't. I have breakfast at seven thirty.

9 (CD1 56) (About Me) **Listen and answer.**

10 (About Me) **Ask and answer with two friends.**

What time do you go to school?

I go to school at nine o'clock.

So do I.

I don't. I go to school at eight thirty.

Remember!

What time do you get up?
I get up at seven o'clock.
So do I.   I don't.

11 (CD1 57) **Go to page 102. Listen and repeat the chant.**

Skills: *Reading and speaking*

Let's start! **Do you have a healthy lifestyle?**

12 (CD1 58) **Read and listen. Then answer the questionnaire.**

		A	B
1	Do you get up early?	Yes, I do.	No, I don't.
2	Do you have breakfast every day?	Yes, I do.	No, I don't.
3	Do you brush your teeth in the morning and in the evening?	Yes, I do.	No, I don't.
4	Do you walk or ride your bike to school?	Yes, I do.	No, I don't.
5	Do you play outside with your friends?	Yes, I do.	No, I don't.
6	Do you like eating fruits and vegetables?	Yes, I do.	No, I don't.
7	Do you like drinking water or milk?	Yes, I do.	No, I don't.
8	Do you go to bed early?	Yes, I do.	No, I don't.

Mostly As – Good job! You have a healthy lifestyle.
Mostly Bs – Hmm! What can you do to be more healthy?

13 (About Me) **Now ask and answer with a friend.**

Do you get up early?   Yes, do. I get up at seven thirty.

Writing

➡ Workbook page 41: Write your own questionnaire.

→ Workbook page 42

Listen and repeat. Then act.

| five o'clock | four thirty | nine thirty | eight o'clock |

Excuse me, what time is it, please?

It's eight o'clock.

Thank you.

Say it!

 Listen and repeat.

Blue whales don't chew their food.

blue whales

→ Workbook page 43   Function: Asking the time   Pronunciation: *ue / ew / oo*   **53**

What time is it around the world?

London 12:00

Dubai 15:00

Shanghai 19:00

Buenos Aires 08:00

1 CD1 62 **Listen and repeat.**

12:00

twelve o'clock

16:15

sixteen fifteen

10:30

ten thirty

23:45

twenty-three forty-five

2 **Watch the video.**

3 **Match the pictures with the cities on page 54. What time is it?**

Guess What!

Brazil has three different time zones.

Project

5 **Make a time chart of your day.**

I get up at 7:00. I eat lunch at 13:15. I play tennis at 15:45. I read my book in bed at 20:30.

4 **What time is it in your country?**

Review
Units 3 and 4

1 Find the words in the puzzles and match to the photographs.

g* t* b*d

h*v* br**kf*st

pl*y t*nn*s

g* t* *rt cl*b

2 (CD1 63) Listen and say the numbers.

3 Read Clara's sentences and say *true* or *false*.

1 I have eggs for breakfast.
2 I play soccer with my friends.
3 I have art club in the afternoon.
4 I go to bed at home.

4 Make your own word puzzles for your friend.

Choose days of the week or daily activities:
S*nd*y
T**sd*y

Clara

1

2

3

4

→ Workbook pages 46–47

Finish

Yellow
What time do you (get up)?
I (get up) at (seven thirty).

Green
What do you have on (Monday) in the (morning)?
I have (English) at (nine o'clock).

Home time

Guess What!

59

1 (CD2 02) **Listen and point.**

2 (CD2 03) **Listen, point, and repeat.**

3 (CD2 04) **Listen and answer the questions.**

1. Is he drinking juice?   Yes, he is.

4 (Think) **Describe and guess the numbers.**

She's making a cake.   Number 9!

1. drink juice
2. eat a sandwich
3. do the dishes
4. play on the computer
5. read a book
6. watch TV
7. do homework
8. listen to music
9. make a cake
10. wash the car

5 CD2 05 **Sing the song.**

We are all different,
In my family.
We are all different,
My family and me.

I like listening to music,
But I don't like reading books.
My mom loves reading books,
But she doesn't like watching TV.

My sister enjoys watching TV,
But she doesn't like making cakes.
My dad loves making cakes,
But he doesn't like listening to music.

6 **Make sentences about the song and say who.**

He enjoys listening to music.   Alex!

7 About Me **Ask and answer with your friend. Then tell another friend.**

Do you like playing on the computer?

Ellie loves playing on the computer.

Yes, I do. I love playing on the computer.

Remember!

He **likes** listening to music.
He **doesn't like** reading books.
She **enjoys** watching TV.
She **loves** playing on the computer.

→ Workbook page 49   Grammar **61**

8 (CD2 06) **Look at the photographs and choose. Then listen and repeat.**

1

Does he like playing on the computer?
Yes, he does. / No, he doesn't.

2

Does she enjoy washing the car?
Yes, she does. / No, she doesn't.

9 (CD2 07) **Listen and find. Then answer the question.**

Pedro

Vivian

Fred

Lina

Anil

Camilla

10 **Ask and answer with a friend.**

Does Lina like doing homework?

Yes, she does.

11 (CD2 08) **Go to page 103. Listen and repeat the chant.**

Remember!

Does he **enjoy** doing the dishes?
Yes, he **does.**   No, he **doesn't.**

Skills: *Listening and speaking*

Let's start! **Are you helpful at home?**

12 (CD2 09) **Listen and choose.**

1 Isabella likes / doesn't like cleaning her bedroom.
2 She enjoys / doesn't enjoy washing the car.
3 She likes / doesn't like doing the dishes.
4 Brad likes / doesn't like cleaning his bedroom.
5 He enjoys / doesn't enjoy washing his bike.
6 He enjoys / doesn't enjoy making cakes.

Brad

Isabella

13 (About Me) **Ask and answer with a friend.**

Do you like cleaning your bedroom?
Do you like washing the car?
Do you like doing the dishes?
Do you like making cakes?

Writing

→ Workbook page 51: Write about being helpful at home.

15 **(Talk Time) Listen and repeat. Then act.**

chocolate cake   cheese sandwich   carrot cake
sausage sandwich   chicken sandwich

1

Let's make a carrot cake.

What do we need?

Eggs, milk, carrots …

OK. Here we are.

2

Let's make a chicken sandwich.

What do we need?

Bread, chicken …

Say it!

16 **Listen and repeat.**

Panthers learn to hunt three months after birth.

panthers

Where do people live?

1 (CD2 13) **Listen and repeat.**

1

2

3

4

countryside   village   town   city

2 **Watch the video.**

3 **What can you see in the pictures?**

1

2

3

4

Guess What!

There are more chickens in the world than people.

Project

5 Make a mind map for a town or a city.

4 **Where would you like to live?**

6 Hobbies

Guess What!

69

1 🔊 CD2 14 Listen and point.

2 🔊 CD2 15 Listen, point, and repeat.

Weekend Clubs and Activities

music clubs
craft clubs
sports clubs

3 🔊 CD2 16 Listen and say the numbers.

4 Think Ask questions and guess the numbers.

Is he playing the piano?   No, he isn't.

Is he making a model?   Yes, he is.

Number 4!

1 play the piano
2 play the guitar
3 play the recorder
4 make models
5 make movies
6 do karate
7 do gymnastics
8 play Ping-Pong
9 play badminton
10 play volleyball

5 (CD2 17) **Sing the song.**

This is our friend Lizzie.
She's very busy!

She plays badminton on Saturdays,
And she does karate on Sundays.
She makes models after school on Wednesdays,
And she makes movies on Mondays.

She doesn't play on the computer,
And she doesn't watch TV after school.
She plays the guitar in the morning,
And she plays the piano in the afternoon.

We like our friend Lizzie.
She's very busy!

6 **Make sentences about the song. Say _true_ or _false_.**

Lizzie doesn't play badminton on Saturdays.   False!

7 (About Me) **Ask and answer with your friend. Then tell another friend.**

Do you do karate?

Yes, I do. I do karate on Saturdays.

Sam does karate on Saturdays.

Remember!

She **does** karate on Sundays.
She **doesn't watch** TV after school.
She **plays** the guitar in the morning.

Look and choose. Then listen and repeat.

1

Jimmy –
Don't forget tennis club on Tuesday.

Does he play tennis on Tuesdays?
Yes, he does. / No, he doesn't.

2

Leah – Remember volleyball club after school.

Does she play volleyball in the morning?
Yes, she does. / No, she doesn't.

 Listen and answer the questions.

Karate club

every Sunday morning

Jimmy

Don't forget recorder club on Tuesday after school

Movie club on Friday afternoons

Don't forget guitar club on Wednesday after school

Bike club on Sunday mornings

Ping-Pong CLUB

every Saturday evening

Leah

 Ask and answer about your friends.

Does George do karate after school?

Yes, he does.

 Go to page 103. Listen and repeat the chant.

Remember!

Does she do gymnastics in the evening?
Yes, she does.   No, she doesn't.

Skills: *Reading and speaking*

 Let's start! **What sports do you like?**

12 (CD2 21) **Read and listen. Then match.**

Sports we like

Meet Josh. He's ten years old, and he wants to be a soccer player.

Josh goes to a soccer club on Tuesdays and Thursdays after school. He plays soccer on Saturdays and Sundays, too. Josh also plays basketball, and he goes swimming.

Josh has a healthy diet. His favorite dinner is chicken with potatoes or rice and vegetables. He likes fruit, too. His favorite drink is a banana milkshake!

13 **Read again and answer the questions.**

1 What club does Josh go to?
2 Does he play soccer on Saturdays?
3 Does he play other sports?
4 Does he eat fruits and vegetables?

14 (About Me) **Ask and answer with a friend.**

Do you go to a club after school?
What sports do you play?
Do you have a healthy diet?
Which fruits and vegetables do you like?

Writing

➜ Workbook page 59: Write about your favorite sport.

CD2 22 **Read and listen.**

→ Workbook page 60

16 CD2 23 Talk Time **Listen and repeat. Then act.**

play the guitar   make models   do gymnastics
do karate   play Ping-Pong

Do you want to play Ping-Pong with me?

No, sorry. I can't play Ping-Pong.

Come on – try it!

OK.

 # Say it!

  17 CD2 24 **Listen and repeat.**

Sharks are fish with sharp teeth.

shark

What type of **musical instrument** is it?

1 CD2 25 **Listen and repeat.**

1

2

3

4

5

brass   percussion   string   woodwind   piano

2 **Watch the video.**

3 **What type of musical instruments can you see?**

4 **What type of instrument would you like to play?**

Guess What!

A piano is a string instrument and a percussion instrument.

Project

5 **Make a drum from recycled cardboard.**

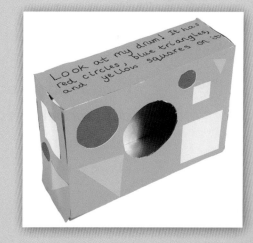

Units 5 and 6

1 Find the words in the puzzles and match to the photographs.

> od scitsanmyg

> yalp llabyellov

> tae a hciwdnas

> netsil ot cisum

Kiki

2 (CD2 26) Listen and say the names.

3 Read and say the names.

1 She likes listening to music.
2 He goes to gymnastics club on Tuesdays.
3 She plays volleyball after school.
4 He likes eating sandwiches.

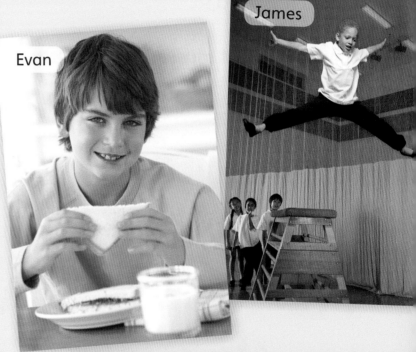

Evan

James

4 Make your own word puzzles for your friend.

> Choose indoor or outdoor activities:
> hsaw eht rac
> ekam a ekac

Clara

→ Workbook pages 64–65

5 Play the game.

79

Guess What!

1 CD2 27 **Listen and point.**

2 CD2 28 **Listen, point, and repeat.**

3 CD2 29 **Listen and say the fruits and vegetables.**

4 Think **Describe and guess what.**

These fruits are small and yellow.   Lemons!

1 lemons
2 limes
3 watermelons
4 coconuts
5 grapes
6 mangoes
7 pineapples
8 pears
9 tomatoes
10 onions

5 **CD2 30** **Sing the song.**

Come and buy some fruit
At my market stall today!

There are lots of pineapples,
And there are some pears,
But there aren't any mangoes
At your market stall today.

Come and buy some fruit
At my market stall today!

There are lots of lemons,
And there are some limes,
But there aren't any tomatoes
At your market stall today.

6 **Look at the song and find the differences in this picture.**

There are lots of grapes.

7 **About Me** **Say what you can buy in your town market.**

There are lots of lemons in my town market.

Remember!
There are lots of grapes.
There are some tomatoes.
There aren't any limes.

8 (CD2 31) **Listen and repeat.**

Are there any onions?

Yes, there are.

Are there any coconuts?

No, there aren't.

9 (Think) **Look at the picture. Then cover it and play a memory game.**

mangoes
coconuts
apples
pineapples
watermelons
carrots
onions
beans
limes
lemons
pears
tomatoes

Are there any mangoes?   No, there aren't.

10 (About Me) **Ask and answer about your classroom.**

Are there any books?   Yes, there are.

Remember!

Are there any pears?
Yes, there are.
No, there aren't.

11 (CD2 32) **Go to page 103. Listen and repeat the chant.**

Skills: *Listening and speaking*

Let's start! **Do you like smoothies?**

12 CD2 33 **Listen and say the numbers.**

1
Mango Cooler with ...
Banana
Mango
Orange juice

2
Tropical Mix with ...
Pineapple
Banana
Orange juice

3
Tutti Frutti with ...
Pineapple
Grapes
Watermelon

Smoothie café

13 CD2 33 **Listen again and answer the questions.**

1 Does Emilio like bananas?
2 What are Arianna's favorite fruit?
3 Does Marco like orange juice?

14 About Me **Ask and answer with a friend.**

What is your favorite smoothie?
What is your favorite fruit?
Which smoothie don't you like?
Which fruit don't you like?

Writing

→ Workbook page 69: Write about your favorite smoothie.

Read and listen.

86 Value: Reuse old things

→ Workbook page 70

16 CD2 35 Talk Time **Listen and repeat. Then act.**

brown watch   red purse   blue guitar   white radio

Which watch do you want?

The brown one, please.

OK. Here you are.

Say it!

17 CD2 36 **Listen and repeat.**

Chipmunks have big cheek pouches.

chipmunk

What parts of
plants
can we eat?

1 (CD2 37) **Listen and repeat.**

2 **Watch the video.**

3 **Match the fruits and vegetables with the plant parts.**

5 fruit

4 leaf

3 stem

2 root

1 seed

roots
stems
leaves
fruit
seeds

Guess What!

Some plants eat small frogs and lizards.

Project

5 **Write a menu using the five parts of plants we can eat.**

Starter

Main

Leaf stem root

Dessert

fruit

4 **What plants do you like to eat?**

Guess What!

1 **Listen and point.**

2 **Listen, point, and repeat.**

3 **Listen and say the words.**

4 **Think** **Make sentences and guess what.**

Lucas is wearing these. They're black.   Sunglasses!

1 sun
2 burger
3 fries
4 sunglasses
5 swimsuit
6 shorts
7 towel
8 shell
9 ocean
10 sand

5 (CD2 41) **Sing the song.**

Which hat is yours?
The red one's mine.
Which hat is yours?
The blue one.

Which sock is hers?
The green one's hers.
Which sock is his?
The yellow one.

Which towel is ours?
The pink one's ours.
Which towel is theirs?
The purple one.

6 **Look at the song. Then read and match.**

1 Which towel is ours?   **2** Which sock is hers?   **3** Which hat is yours?   **4** Which sock is his?   **5** Which towel is theirs?

a The green one's hers.   **b** The yellow one's his.   **c** The blue one's mine.

d The purple one.   **e** The pink one.

7 (About Me) **Ask and answer about your classroom.**

Which pencil case is yours?

The purple one's mine.

Remember!

Which sock is **hers**?
The green **one's hers**.
Which towel is **theirs**?
The purple **one**.

8 CD2 42 Listen and repeat.

Whose jacket is this?

It's mine.

Whose shoes are these?

They're Sally's.

9 About Me Find these things in your classroom. Then ask and answer.

Whose backpack is this?

It's Mark's.

10 CD2 43 Go to page 103. Listen and repeat the chant.

Remember!

Whose glasses are these?
They're mine.

→ Workbook page 76

Skills: *Reading and speaking*

Let's start! **What do you like doing on vacation?**

11 (CD2 44) **Read and listen. Then match.**

a

Dear Grandma and Grandpa,

We're having a great vacation. Can you see the hotel next to the beach? That's ours!

The beach is great. We like playing in the sand. There are lots of shells. We like making pictures with them.

In the evening, we go to the café on the beach. You can see it in this photograph. I like eating a burger and fries. They're delicious!

See you soon!

Love from Louis

b

12 **Read and say *true* or *false*.**

1 Their hotel is next to a forest.
2 They like playing on the beach.
3 There aren't any shells on the beach.
4 Louis likes eating chicken and fries.

13 (About Me) **Ask and answer with a friend.**

Where do you like going on vacation?
Who do you go on vacation with?
What do you do on vacation?
What do you like eating on vacation?

Writing

→ Workbook page 77: Write a postcard to a friend.

15   **Listen and repeat. Then act.**

| by plane | by bike | on foot | by train | by car | by bus |

1

How should we get to the movie theater?

Let's go by car.

OK. Good idea.

2

How should we get to the beach?

Let's go by bus.

No, let's go by train!

Say it!

16   **Listen and repeat.**

Dolphins are friendly and eat fish.

dolphins

Are sea animals symmetrical?